CELEBRATING THE NAME HEATHER

Celebrating the Name Heather

Walter the Educator

Silent King Books

SILENT KING BOOKS

SKB

Copyright © 2024 by Walter the Educator

All rights reserved. No part of this book may be reproduced in any manner whatsoever without written permission except in the case of brief quotations embodied in critical articles and reviews.

First Printing, 2024

Disclaimer
This book is a literary work; poems are not about specific persons, locations, situations, and/or circumstances unless mentioned in a historical context. This book is for entertainment and informational purposes only. The author and publisher offer this information without warranties expressed or implied. No matter the grounds, neither the author nor the publisher will be accountable for any losses, injuries, or other damages caused by the reader's use of this book. The use of this book acknowledges an understanding and acceptance of this disclaimer.

dedicated to everyone with the first name of Heather

HEATHER

Heather blooms with pride,

HEATHER

A maiden fair did softly stride,

HEATHER

Her name, a melody to confide,

HEATHER

In whispers of the winds, it sighed.

HEATHER

Heather, the muse of twilight hues,

HEATHER

In her eyes, the stars would choose

HEATHER

To dance in patterns, never to lose,

HEATHER

In her embrace, the night ensues.

HEATHER

Beneath the veil of azure skies,

HEATHER

Heather's laughter, a sweet surprise,

HEATHER

Echoes through the mountains rise,

HEATHER

In every peak, her essence lies.

HEATHER

A name adorned with nature's grace,

HEATHER

In forests deep, in open space,

HEATHER

Heather's spirit, a gentle embrace,

HEATHER

Wherever she roams, a sacred place.

HEATHER

In whispers heard by silent streams,

HEATHER

Heather's dreams are woven in gleams,

HEATHER

A tapestry of hopes and schemes,

HEATHER

In moonlit nights, she softly deems.

HEATHER

With every step, the earth would sing,

HEATHER

Of Heather's joy, a vibrant spring,

HEATHER

In every bloom, her essence cling,

HEATHER

In every note, her praises ring.

HEATHER

In gardens lush, where flowers sway,

HEATHER

Heather's touch, a tender display,

HEATHER

In every petal, colors array,

HEATHER

In every fragrance, her love's bouquet.

HEATHER

Her name, a beacon in the night,

HEATHER

Guiding lost souls to the light,

HEATHER

In the depths of darkness, taking flight,

HEATHER

Heather's presence, a celestial sight.

HEATHER

In tales of old and legends told,

HEATHER

Heather's name, a treasure to behold,

HEATHER

In whispers carried by winds so bold,

HEATHER

In every saga, her story's told.

HEATHER

So let us raise our voices high,

HEATHER

To Heather's name, let love comply,

HEATHER

In every heart, her spirit fly,

HEATHER

In every soul, her legacy amplify.

HEATHER

For she is more than just a name,

HEATHER

In every breath, her essence claim,

HEATHER

In every verse, her flame's aflame,

HEATHER

In Heather's grace, we find our aim.

HEATHER

ABOUT THE CREATOR

Walter the Educator is one of the pseudonyms for Walter Anderson. Formally educated in Chemistry, Business, and Education, he is an educator, an author, a diverse entrepreneur, and he is the son of a disabled war veteran. "Walter the Educator" shares his time between educating and creating. He holds interests and owns several creative projects that entertain, enlighten, enhance, and educate, hoping to inspire and motivate you.

> Follow, find new works, and stay up to date
> with Walter the Educator™
> at WaltertheEducator.com

www.ingramcontent.com/pod-product-compliance
Lightning Source LLC
LaVergne TN
LVHW020134080526
838201LV00119B/3863